SPOTLIGHT ON
SPECIAL EDUCATIONAL NEEDS:

HEARING IMPAIRMENT

LINDA M. WATSON

A NASEN Publication

Published in 1996
Second Edition 2003

ISBN 0 906730 82 1

Published by NASEN.
NASEN is a registered charity. Charity No. 1007023.
NASEN is a company limited by guarantee, registered in England and Wales. Company No. 2637438.

Further copies of this book and details of NASEN's many other publications may be obtained from the NASEN Bookshop at its registered office: NASEN House, 4/5 Amber Business Village, Amber Close, Amington, Tamworth, Staffs. B77 4RP.
Tel: 01827 311500; Fax: 01827 313005; Email: welcome@nasen.org.uk
Website: www.nasen.org.uk

Copy editing by Nicola von Schreiber.
Cover design by Mark Procter.
Typeset in Times by J. C. Typesetting and printed in the United Kingdom by Stowes, Stoke-on-Trent.

SPOTLIGHT ON SPECIAL EDUCATIONAL NEEDS: HEARING IMPAIRMENT

Contents

Acknowledgements

The authors and publishers gratefully acknowledge permission given by Messrs Connevans Ltd, 54 Albert Road North, Reigate RH2 9YR to reproduce all of the figures in this book related to hearing aids and radio hearing aids; also that of Cochlear to reproduce Figure 12 on page 30.

SPOTLIGHT ON SPECIAL EDUCATIONAL NEEDS: HEARING IMPAIRMENT

Introduction

Hearing impairment in young children is very common. It has been estimated that in any infant class at any one time as many as 20 per cent (or even more in some areas) of pupils will be experiencing some degree of fluctuating hearing difficulty (Bamford and Saunders, 1991). If you add to this number those pupils with permanent hearing losses who are now being integrated into mainstream classes, it is clear that many teachers will encounter pupils with hearing impairment in the course of their work.

This booklet is intended for teachers who are not specialist teachers of the deaf, but who might have pupils with hearing impairment in their classes. It should also prove useful to Special Educational Needs Co-ordinators (SENCOs), classroom assistants, school governors and parents of pupils with hearing impairment.

It has long been the practice for many pupils with hearing impairment to be educated in their local school or in a school with a unit for hearing impaired pupils attached to it. This situation predated the *Education Act 1981,* which introduced the concept of greater integration of pupils with special educational needs into mainstream schools. Indeed, it could be said that Services for Hearing Impaired Pupils were among those who pioneered the integration of pupils with special educational needs into mainstream classes.

The terms 'hearing impaired' and 'deaf' are frequently used interchangeably, although the title 'teacher of the deaf' tends to persist, and some Services for pupils with impaired hearing are reverting to the title of Services for Deaf Pupils. The other situation in which the term Deaf (with a capital D) is used is to denote deaf people who identify with the Deaf community and seek to promote its distinct culture and language. For the purposes of this booklet, it should be understood that the term 'hearing impaired' refers to pupils with hearing losses ranging in severity from mild to profound. These different categories of hearing loss will be defined in a later section.

When seeking to meet the needs of pupils with hearing impairment, the requirements of the *Special Educational Needs Code of Practice* (DfES, 2001) and the new duties from 2002 outlined in the *Disability Discrimination Act 1995 Part 4 Code of Practice for Schools* must be borne in mind. Some implications of these codes for pupils with hearing impairment will be discussed.

Understanding Hearing Loss

How the ear works

It is easiest to think of the ear in three parts: the outer ear, middle ear and inner ear. Figure 1 shows a cross-section of the three parts of the ear.

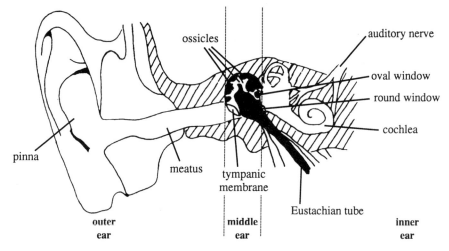

Figure 1 - The ear.

The outer and middle ear are responsible for conducting sound to the inner ear. The outer ear consists of the pinna (the most visible part, which we often refer to as 'the ear') and the ear canal (or auditory meatus) which leads down to the eardrum (or tympanic membrane). The pinna is probably the least significant part of the hearing mechanism, although it does perform the important function of collecting sound and directing it down the ear canal towards the drum. When sound waves reach the eardrum they set it into vibration, and this in turn sets the three bones in the middle ear (the ossicles) into vibration. The middle ear is an air-filled cavity, which means that the ossicles can move freely in the air. The third bone of the ossicular chain (the stapes) is connected to the oval window, which is part of the cochlea (the inner ear). The cochlea is shaped like a snail's shell (hence the name) and contains thick fluid. As the ossicles vibrate, the oval window is set into motion. This excites the fluid in the cochlea which stimulates the hair cells. The movement of the hair cells generates an electrical current which is transmitted along the auditory nerve to the brain where it is perceived as sound.

A hearing loss that originates in either the outer or middle ear, which are responsible for conducting the sound to the inner ear, is known as a *conductive* hearing loss. A hearing loss that arises from a problem in the inner ear or nerve of hearing is referred to as a *sensori-neural* hearing loss, although the old terms 'perceptive' hearing loss or 'nerve' deafness are still sometimes used.

Causes of hearing loss
Problems with the outer ear
Sometimes children are born without a pinna. Provided the other parts of the ear are not affected, this will result in only a minor degree of hearing loss. On occasions the absence of a pinna is accompanied by abnormalities in the middle ear, but the resulting loss is still not usually severe.

The ear canal may become blocked with wax, or obstructed by beads or other small objects which children are prone to push into their ears. Wax may become more of a problem after swimming or bathing when water entering the ear canal causes the wax to swell, thus blocking the ear canal and causing a hearing loss. This may necessitate the removal of the wax, which must be carried out by a qualified doctor or nurse. Attempts to remove wax by inserting an implement (such as a pin, hairgrip or cotton bud) into the ear can result in damage to the eardrum as the wax may be pushed further down the canal. This practice should therefore be discouraged.

Middle ear problems
Problems in the middle ear may be congenital (ie present from birth). The three bones, known as the ossicles (see Figure 1), may be malformed. However, the most common middle ear problem experienced by children, and the type of hearing loss most frequently encountered by mainstream teachers, is that which arises from the condition known as 'glue ear'. In this condition the Eustachian tube (see Figure 1), which runs from the back of the throat to the middle ear, becomes blocked, often following a cold or ear infection. The Eustachian tube usually opens when we yawn or swallow, to allow air to enter the middle ear cavity. When this cavity is filled with air the pressure on either side of the eardrum is equal, which keeps the drum taut and ensures that it vibrates easily. When the Eustachian tube gets blocked, air cannot enter the middle ear cavity. First a negative pressure results, which means that the drum is no longer held taut but is drawn inwards, then fluid seeps into the middle ear cavity from the lining of the middle ear. While this fluid remains thin and watery, there is a chance that it will drain away when the Eustachian tube clears, and the state of the middle ear, and with it the child's hearing, will return to normal.

7

However, sometimes the fluid becomes thick and glue-like in quality, hence the name 'glue ear'. This thick fluid is less likely to clear of its own accord, and surgical treatment may be called for. The fluid can cause a moderate degree of hearing loss since the eardrum cannot move so freely to conduct sound to the ossicles, neither can the ossicles move as easily as normal since they are having to move in fluid rather than in air.

An ear, nose and throat (ENT) consultant may decide to operate to remove the fluid. The surgeon may simply make a small incision in the eardrum and suck out the fluid. This operation is called a *myringotomy*. While performing a myringotomy, the surgeon may decide to insert a tiny grommet in the eardrum to keep a hole in it for a while to allow air to enter the middle ear cavity through the grommet to compensate for the blocked Eustachian tube. Grommets usually work their own way out of the drum over a period of weeks or months, but occasionally they need to be removed surgically. Some children need to have grommets inserted two or three times because of recurrent problems.

A child with grommets should be allowed to participate fully in PE and games, but should only be allowed to go swimming with the agreement of the consultant. Some consultants allow children with grommets to swim, while others are opposed. In some children who are prone to middle ear problems, the chemicals in the water at the swimming pool seem to aggravate the problem. The ears of a child with grommets should not discharge. Any child whose ears are discharging should be referred for medical advice.

ENT consultants vary in their approach to intervention for glue ear. While some consultants are happy to perform surgery and even repeat it two or three times, others prefer to wait and see whether the problem clears itself, since children usually grow out of it. The necessity to operate more than once may not be desirable and, in rare cases, can cause scarring of the drum. Teachers need to understand that, in the longer term, an operation may not be the best solution for a particular pupil, although it may seem to offer a quick answer.

The degree of hearing loss experienced by a child with glue ear will vary, both from child to child and sometimes in the same child from day to day. This can add to the difficulties experienced both by the child and by those with whom the child comes into contact. The effects can be that normal conversation is heard as a whisper, or speech may sound muffled.

Some children do not seem to be too disadvantaged by the hearing loss in educational terms, managing to function well in spite of their hearing difficulty. As long as people gain their attention before talking to them and raise their voices slightly then these children are able to cope in spite of their hearing loss. However, for others the effects can be very serious. These are often, although not always, those children who are already disadvantaged by other difficulties.

Possible effects of a hearing loss resulting from glue ear
The child:

• does not respond to being called by name;

• may hear (and therefore respond to) only part of a message;

• may hear better in some conditions than others (for example, may hear well in a small room, but not in a large hall);

• may hear well on some days but not so well on others;

• may have difficulty in hearing against background noise;

• may have difficulty in hearing the difference between similar sounds (for example, 'cat/hat' or 't/d' in phonic work);

• may display unacceptable behaviour during lessons that require children to listen, as listening is a difficult and therefore frustrating task for them.

These hearing difficulties mean that the child has to concentrate and really listen all the time in order to hear. This is exhausting and so it is no wonder that at times many of these children 'switch off' and stop listening or paying attention. This can lead to more generalised difficulties in learning as poor learning habits become established.

In order to help such children, the teacher should:
• provide good listening conditions (for example, keep background noise to a minimum, try to work with these children in a quiet area of the room);

• encourage them to position themselves close to the teacher;

• create conditions so that children can lip-read easily:
  – do not stand with your back to the window
  – do not keep moving about
  – speak clearly without exaggerating your lip patterns
  – work at the children's level;

• provide breaks from listening;

> - not stress detailed listening work (for example, phonics) when it is obvious that the child is not hearing well;
>
> - provide opportunities for success.

There are also some useful strategies for teachers to employ once the pupil's hearing has returned to normal. These strategies are often ignored, with the result that the pupil may continue to act as if he or she has a hearing impairment. Since hearing and listening are two different activities, it is important that listening is encouraged once hearing has returned to normal.

For further reading about pupils with conductive hearing impairment, see Watson, Gregory and Powers (1999).

> In addition, once the child has undergone an operation, or testing shows that hearing has returned to normal, the teacher should:
>
> - encourage careful listening, in quiet conditions at first;
>
> - reward responses to sounds, especially quieter sounds;
>
> - work on developing listening skills, for example by playing listening games;
>
> - give the child confidence that he or she can now hear better.

Such strategies could expect to be provided under the banner of Early Years Action or School Action in relation to the *SEN Code of Practice,* although it is a topic that could usefully be addressed in INSET provided by an external specialist, for example a visiting teacher of the deaf, so might be described as Early Years Action Plus or School Action Plus.

Some behavioural difficulties in older pupils may have their roots in early hearing difficulties which were not managed sensitively and resulted in the establishment of poor learning habits, although this is difficult to prove.

Problems with the inner ear or beyond

A problem arising in the inner ear (known as the cochlea) or in the auditory nerve will result in a sensori-neural hearing loss. While some conductive hearing losses may right themselves spontaneously or be treatable by surgical intervention, as mentioned above, there is no cure for sensori-neural hearing losses.

The cochlea is shaped like a snail's shell. It contains thick fluid and tiny hair cells. It is these hair cells that are susceptible to damage. This can occur during pregnancy. Some illnesses contracted by the mother, such as rubella, can cross the placenta and cause damage to the unborn child. If the infant or child contracts certain illnesses, such as meningitis, the cochlea can suffer damage, either resulting from the disease itself or from lifesaving drugs used to treat it. Alternatively, the cochlea may not develop properly in the womb.

It is worth considering briefly the various causes of sensori-neural hearing loss, since the aetiology (cause) may be associated with other difficulties in addition to hearing loss. Sensori-neural losses are often considered in three groups, relating to the time of onset: prenatal, perinatal and post-natal (or acquired) hearing loss.

Prenatal causes

A child may be born with a hearing loss, either by inheriting it or resulting from damage in the womb. For many such children the aetiology is not known. While genetic counselling may reveal a history of hearing loss in the family which had hitherto gone unrecognised, it may not be possible to say for certain what has caused the hearing problem. In the absence of any other explanation, it is often assumed that it has resulted from a recessive gene in both parents. In other words, that both parents carry a gene for deafness, but since they only have one affected gene neither parent has a hearing loss. However, when they produce children there is a chance (approximately 1:4) that any of the children may inherit a gene for deafness from each parent, giving two genes for deafness with a resultant hearing loss.

It can be frustrating for a hearing impaired teenager or young adult not to know the cause of the hearing impairment since it makes it difficult to predict whether there is a likelihood that any children they have might have a hearing impairment.

German measles (rubella) contracted by the mother during pregnancy used to be a common cause of hearing loss in children. The damage was often not restricted to the ears, and the child could be born with visual impairment, heart defects, learning difficulties or any combination of these. The practice of immunising teenage girls, and more recently all babies, against rubella has resulted in a sharp decline in babies born damaged by the disease.

Perinatal causes

Perinatal causes are associated with a difficult birth history resulting in lack of oxygen, or with very low birth weight and the problems associated with this. Hearing impairment may be only one of several handicaps suffered by the baby.

11

Post-natal causes

The commonest cause of post-natal or acquired hearing loss in children is meningitis, which can lead to a very profound loss of hearing – in some cases the child becomes totally deaf. Other viral illnesses, for example measles and mumps, can also cause hearing loss. A loss resulting from mumps tends to affect only one ear and may go undetected for some time. All these diseases cause damage to the hair cells in the cochlea (see above). It is to be hoped that new immunisation routines will reduce hearing loss resulting from these causes, as it has already done with rubella.

Accidents or other forms of trauma may give rise to a hearing loss, and there is some evidence that exposure to excessive levels of noise over long periods may lead to hearing loss in later life (Reed, 1984).

Unilateral hearing loss

Some children are born with a hearing loss in one ear, with normal hearing in the other. This is known as a unilateral or monaural (ie affecting one ear) loss. As just mentioned, other pupils develop this type of loss following mumps. A loss in one ear does not reduce the ability to hear by 50 per cent. Provided that the pupil is listening in good listening conditions, positioned so that the better ear is facing the source of the sound, they should not be very disadvantaged. A unilateral hearing loss goes undetected in some pupils for a long time. A few pupils, however, do seem to be more disadvantaged by a unilateral loss.

Possible effects of a unilateral hearing loss
The pupil:

• finds difficulty in locating the source of a sound;

• may turn the wrong way when called;

• may find it difficult to hear in noisy conditions;

• may fail to hear if addressed on their deaf side;

• may find difficulty in listening via a tape recorder.

For further information, see Watson et al. (1999). There are a few useful strategies which should be implemented by teachers who are teaching pupils with unilateral hearing loss.

> **Strategies for helping pupils with unilateral hearing loss**
> - Ensure that the pupil is seated with the deaf ear towards a wall or window and the good ear facing the class.
>
> - Encourage the pupil to watch as well as listen.
>
> - Reduce levels of background noise.
>
> - Give extra attention to road safety procedures, especially if the pupil rides a bike (a rear view mirror attached to the handle bars may be beneficial, particularly if the loss is in the right ear which is the ear that faces traffic).
>
> - Provide good quality sound reproducing equipment if using audio cassettes or radio.
>
> - Seek advice if giving careers guidance as a few careers require normal hearing in both ears.

Such strategies could expect to be provided in the context of Early Years Action or School Action. However, if external agencies are involved in road safety training or educational visits, it is important that they are informed of the pupil's unilateral loss (with the permission of the pupil and parents) as there could be safety implications. Should the parent or pupil ask for the existence of the unilateral hearing loss to be kept confidential, the school could take the decision that, for the sake of the child's safety, the child should not be allowed to participate in the activity. The *Disability Discrimination Act Code of Practice for Schools* suggests that such an action on the part of the school would be likely to be considered lawful if it were challenged.

Mixed losses

Some children who already have a sensori-neural hearing loss may develop a conductive hearing loss (glue ear) as well. Pupils with a sensori-neural loss usually have their hearing tested regularly and are examined to ensure that a conductive hearing loss is not present as its effects can be very severe on a pupil with a pre-existing sensori-neural loss. Since conductive hearing loss is so common in young children, the probability of a hearing impaired pupil developing a conductive hearing loss on top of the sensori-neural loss is quite high. In this case the pupil is described as having a 'mixed' loss (ie a mixture of conductive and sensori-neural) or as having a 'conductive overlay' on top of a sensori-neural loss.

Central deafness

For some pupils with hearing loss the cause lies not in the conductive pathway, the cochlea or the auditory nerve, but rather it is the brain that fails to respond normally to sound. This type of deafness, known as *central deafness*, is difficult to treat.

Functional hearing loss

Occasionally a pupil may present with a hearing loss that has no pathological basis. This pupil is described as having a *functional* hearing loss (sometimes called a non-organic or psychogenic loss). It is usually possible for a skilled audiologist to demonstrate that the hearing is actually normal, but clearly the pupil will be in need of other help.

Assessment of Hearing

The assessment of hearing is concerned in the first instance with determining whether or not the hearing falls within the normal range. This is usually determined by the administration of some form of screening test.

Screening tests of hearing

A screening test of hearing is designed to pick out those children who may have a problem for more detailed investigation, while allowing those with hearing within normal limits to pass the test. It is now possible to screen babies for possible hearing loss immediately after birth and newborn hearing screening programmes are gradually being introduced throughout the country. The test most commonly used involves placing a small probe in the baby's ear and feeding a sound into the ear canal. In a healthy ear, the cochlea (see Figure 1 on page 6) produces an echo that is registered via the probe. If the echo is present, it suggests that the cochlea (the most common site of permanent hearing loss) is healthy. This test, which is quick to administer and painless for the baby, can detect the majority of hearing losses that are present at birth. It is known as an oto-acoustic emissions test (OAE).

If a newborn screening test is not used, babies are screened for hearing at around 8 months of age. This is an age by which the majority of babies are able to sit on an adult's lap unsupported and turn their head freely from side to side. The test, which is known as the distraction test, requires two skilled operators. One tester distracts the baby's attention while the other tester introduces sounds behind the baby's head to either side, out of the line of vision, and watches for the baby to turn their head to the source of the sound. While it may appear to be a very simple test, it requires a considerable amount of skill, but if performed properly it can pick out those babies whose hearing status requires further investigation.

The timing for routine screening varies from area to area, but in most areas a second screen will take place either before entry to school or soon after. This will take the form of an audiogram (see below).

Diagnostic tests

If a child fails a screening test or there is reason to suspect a hearing loss, more detailed investigations will be carried out. The purpose of these tests is to discover whether there is a hearing loss present, and if so the precise nature and extent of the loss.

It will be important to differentiate between a conductive loss and a sensori-neural loss, as described above (see Understanding Hearing Loss), so that any appropriate treatment can be given for a conductive loss. There are tests of the middle ear function which will assist in differential diagnosis between these conditions.

In addition to the type of loss, there are two other parameters of interest: the extent of the loss (ie how loud sounds need to be for the child to hear them) and whether the loss is the same for all sounds. For many people with hearing impairment the loss is not equal for all sounds – they can hear some sounds much better than others. Often they can hear low frequency sounds (ie low pitched sounds) better than high frequency sounds. The implications of this will be explained in detail below.

The pure tone audiogram

The pure tone audiogram is the most widely used hearing test. It tests the adult's or child's ability to hear individual sounds (pure tones) at different intensities, measured in decibels (dB) and at different frequencies (ie low and high pitched sounds). The frequencies that are tested are those that are important for detecting the components of speech. The lowest sound measured is 250 Hertz (Hz), or cycles per second (for comparative purposes Middle C is 261 Hz), while the highest sound is four, or sometimes five, octaves above this. The results of the test are plotted on a graph (the audiogram). Zero on the graph represents the level at which a young person with 'normal' hearing can just detect the sound, so it really means 'no hearing loss'. It is presented as a straight line on the graph, but in reality the intensity at which the ear can just detect sounds varies from frequency to frequency. A response at or better than 20 dB is usually considered to be within normal limits. Figure 2 shows the standard audiogram form.

The pure tone audiogram may be used as a screening test, with all sounds presented at one level (usually around 20 dB) with the child expected to respond at each frequency. If the child responds to each of the frequencies tested at this level, it is assumed that hearing is within normal limits. In practical terms it is assumed that the pupil can hear sufficiently well to detect all the sounds of speech and to function without difficulty in the classroom situation. There is research, however, that suggests that some individual children whose hearing levels are just above the level tested in screening can still experience sufficient difficulty in hearing clearly for this to interfere with their performance in school (Bamford and Saunders, 1991).

The pure tone audiogram is also used as a diagnostic test of hearing, to reveal the degree of hearing loss at each frequency. Figures 3–6 show four examples of audiograms. Figure 3 is an example of hearing that is within normal limits, while Figures 4–6 are examples of different types of hearing loss.

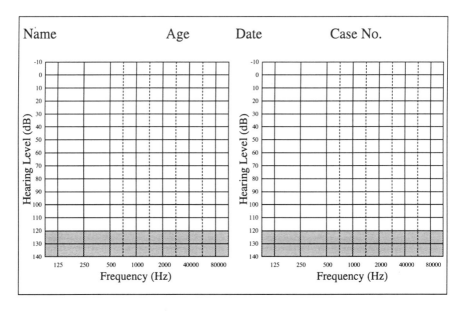

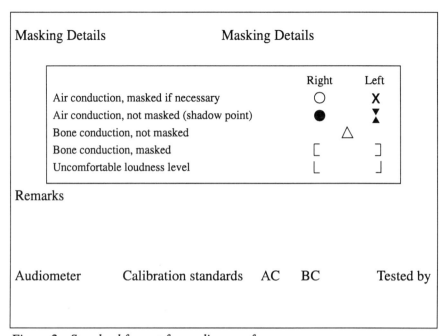

Masking Details   Masking Details

	Right	Left
Air conduction, masked if necessary	○	X
Air conduction, not masked (shadow point)	●	▼▲
Bone conduction, not masked	△	
Bone conduction, masked	[	]
Uncomfortable loudness level	L	⌐

Remarks

Audiometer   Calibration standards   AC   BC   Tested by

Figure 2 - Standard format for audiogram form.

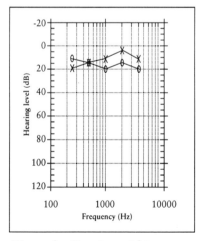

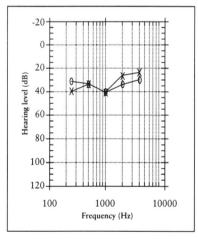

Figure 3 - Hearing within   *Figure 4 - A flat loss.*
*   normal limits.*

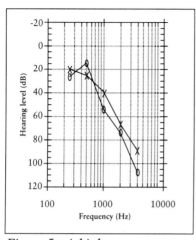

*Figure 5 - A high
frequency loss.*

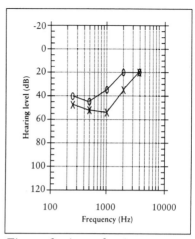

*Figure 6 - A conductive
loss – glue ear.*

Interpreting audiograms

The results for the right ear are entered on the audiogram as an 0, while those for the left are entered as an x. They may be recorded on two separate graphs, or both on the same one. Sometimes they are also colour coded: red for the right ear and black or blue for the left. The results for low frequency sounds (ie low pitched sounds, predominantly vowels) are on the left of the graph, and those for high frequency sounds (mainly consonants) are on the right. The further down the graph the results are, the more severe the hearing loss. If all the results for both ears are at the top of the graph, above the 20dB line, then hearing is said to be within normal limits (see Figure 3).

Different types of hearing loss

Flat loss

A hearing loss may be roughly equivalent for each frequency, in which case it is known as a 'flat' loss (see Figure 4). The further down the graph the results, the more severe the loss. A typical conductive hearing loss is either flat or may be more severe for the low frequencies (see Figure 6).

High frequency loss

If the results are within, or close to, normal limits for the low frequencies (ie on the left-hand side of the audiogram), but show a loss for the high frequencies (ie on the right-hand side of the audiogram), this indicates a high frequency loss (see Figure 5). This can occur in one or both ears.

18

The consonant sounds of speech are high frequency sounds. In running speech, it is the consonant sounds that carry the most information. It is easy to understand 'Jack and Jill went up the hill' from the consonants:

Jk nd Jll wnt p th hll

but much more difficult from the vowels alone:

a a i e u e i

Unfortunately, not only are the consonant sounds mostly high frequency sounds, they also tend to be produced with less intensity than vowel sounds, making them quieter. This means that the pupil may well hear that something has been said, but hear it imperfectly, having heard mainly the vowel sounds. This can be very frustrating for the hearing impaired person who may think that the speaker has not spoken clearly, and may try to fill in what has not been heard using guesswork. The speaker, on the other hand, may consider that since the hearing impaired person has obviously heard something then they are guilty of not listening properly. The child (or adult, as this is precisely the type of loss that develops with old age) with this type of hearing impairment can often be accused of 'hearing when they want to', when the reality is that their ability to hear speech depends on several factors – it is likely to vary depending on listening conditions and the familiarity of the language addressed to the child, as well as on whether or not the child is actually listening. It also demands great concentration to listen continually and it is difficult to sustain this level of concentration for long periods.

Conductive loss
A conductive loss resulting from glue ear frequently affects the lower frequencies more severely than the higher ones (see Figure 6). The effects of this different type of hearing impairment are discussed above (see Understanding Hearing Loss).

Unilateral loss
If the results for one ear are within normal limits, but those for the other show a hearing loss, then this is described as a unilateral (or monaural) hearing loss. This may occur in either ear, and may be mild, moderate, severe or profound in degree.

19

If the result is blocked in on the audiogram (see legend for Figure 2) this means that it may not be a true result for that ear, but rather what is referred to as a 'shadow curve'. The reason for this is that when testing an ear with a hearing loss it is possible for the sound to be heard in the 'good' ear rather than in the one being tested. This happens because the sound sets the bones of the skull into vibration and so the sound is transmitted to the other ear by bone conduction. In order to obtain a true reading for the ear being tested, it is necessary for a noise to be introduced into the good ear to prevent the sound from being detected in the good ear by mistake. This procedure is known as masking. If, due to lack of time or the fact that the child is too immature to cope with it, masking is not used, then the blocked symbol is entered on the chart to indicate that it may not be a true reading. Figure 7 is an example of a unilateral loss in the right ear. The levels recorded may not be a true reading. It is possible that the pupil has no useful hearing in the right ear (sometimes referred to as a 'dead ear'.)

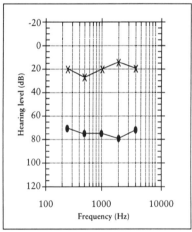

Figure 7 - Unilateral loss showing a possible shadow curve.

Average hearing loss

For ease of description, the average hearing loss is often quoted. This is calculated by averaging the values for the five frequencies that are considered most important for hearing speech (250 Hz, 500 Hz, 1 kHz, 2 kHz and 4 kHz) in the better ear, taking no account of the loss in the other ear. The actual value may then be quoted, or alternatively the category into which it falls may be given. There are four categories:

20

Mild hearing loss	up to 40 dB
Moderate hearing loss	41–70 dB
Severe hearing loss	71–95 dB
Profound hearing loss	over 95 dB

In practical terms, pupils with a mild loss are likely to miss some individual speech sounds and mishear some words. This can lead to immaturities in speech development and difficulties with phonics.

A pupil with a moderate loss will probably have difficulty in comprehending speech at normal conversational voice level unless they are able to supplement their hearing with lip-reading. However, in good listening conditions, if they are close to the person speaking and, if appropriate, have the benefit of a suitable hearing aid they may hear well.

For pupils with severe or profound losses the effects are variable. They will not be able to hear conversation without the aid of hearing aids, and, without the use of hearing aids, even a clap of thunder overhead may be inaudible, but a jet engine at close range may be heard (or possibly felt). For these pupils it is impossible to make generalisations on what they will be able to hear or how well they will be able to make use of their residual hearing. Meaningful discussion can only take place at an individual level.

Aided thresholds

For a pupil who is fitted with hearing aids, the audiogram may be repeated while the pupil is wearing the hearing aids and the results plotted on the audiogram. These results are referred to as *aided thresholds*. There is no standardised format for recording these results, but they are often entered on the pure tone audiogram form, indicated by A (for aided).

To carry out this test the pupil cannot wear headphones on top of hearing aids, so a calibrated soundfield set-up is required. The advantage of this test is that it demonstrates the improvement in hearing threshold which the pupil gains from the hearing aids. This is important information since some pupils are able to make more use of the hearing they have (their residual hearing) than others. This depends on several factors, including age at diagnosis and fitting of hearing aids and encouragement to listen as well as factors within the child.

Other tests

There are other investigations that are often carried out on babies and young children when a hearing loss is suspected, which do not involve active co-operation on the part of the child. Some tests can be performed on very young babies when there is the possibility of a congenital hearing loss, for example where there is a family history of deafness. This means that babies can be diagnosed very early. Once a hearing loss has been diagnosed, the family will receive regular support from a teacher of the deaf to assist them in promoting the child's communication skills, listening skills and other aspects of development. The benefits of early diagnosis should be obvious by the time the child starts school in the relative amount of progress that the child has made.

Hearing for speech

While the audiogram gives information on the pupil's ability to hear individual sounds, it does not detail precisely how well that pupil can detect speech, which is composed of sounds of many different frequencies. In order to discover how well a pupil can hear speech, speech tests of hearing are often used. In these tests, the pupil is expected either to select different toys or pictures on request, or to repeat words. They can be useful tests for demonstrating to the class teacher, for example, the nature of the pupil's difficulties. However, they do depend on the pupil knowing the names of the toys or knowing the words that are being presented, so may not be suitable for pupils with language difficulties.

Young children are asked to select small toys from a group of toys. For one test which is widely used (the McCormick Toy Test), there are 14 toys, which are in seven pairs that sound alike (for example, 'cup' and 'duck'). The child is asked to name the toys as they are placed on the table and then to point to different ones. The toys used in the test are:

cup	duck
shoe	spoon
cow	house
fork	horse
tree	key
man	lamb
plane	plate

A child with a hearing impairment may need to hear the words in a raised voice to select the toys accurately. A child with a high frequency loss is likely to confuse some of the pairs, for example to select 'cow' instead of 'house', having heard only the vowel sound clearly.

The test may be used under different conditions, for example with hearing aids and without hearing aids or with lip-reading and without lip-reading, in order to demonstrate how well the child hears in different situations. It can prove to be a good way of showing the benefits of wearing a hearing aid.

Older pupils are asked to repeat either single words or sentences. A list of single words can reveal a pupil's difficulty in hearing the whole of a word. Here is an example of an AB word list, commonly used with older pupils:

ship
rug
fan
cheek
haze
dice
both
well
jot
move

Common mistakes are:

van for fan
cheap for cheek
die for dice
boat for both

This shows how a pupil may mishear a word at the beginning of a lesson and this may cause confusion for them throughout the whole lesson. If a pupil is having difficulty in hearing individual words accurately, then they will need to rely on the context of the sentence to tell them what the word is. Writing key vocabulary on the board or giving explanations of words is extremely helpful.

Speech tests of hearing are sometimes used as a screening test. They are also used with pupils who have been diagnosed as having a hearing impairment to complement results of other tests. They are particularly useful to teachers as they can demonstrate the effects of the hearing impairment in practical terms in school. This is important as the precise effects of a hearing impairment on a pupil are the result of a complex blend of factors, one of which is the extent to which an individual pupil is able to utilise his or her residual hearing. This information is not provided by the pure tone audiogram.

Hearing and listening

Speech tests of hearing, as just described, show the person's ability to hear in different situations. Good acoustic conditions will provide circumstances in which pupils can hear more clearly and will encourage them to attend to what they hear (ie, to listen).

Conditions that aid both hearing and listening
- Rooms with carpets, curtains and soft furnishings;

- acoustic treatment of rooms;

- soft tops on tables, and rubber feet on tables and chairs;

- reducing background noise;

- speaking to a pupil with a hearing impairment from a close range rather than across the room;

- gaining the pupil's attention before speaking;

- good lighting, which makes it easier to use all senses to aid understanding;

- appropriate use of amplification equipment (hearing aids and radio hearing aids).

Acoustic conditions in some schools are much better than in others for pupils with hearing impairment. In general, open plan schools do not provide good listening conditions for pupils with hearing impairment.

Some schools are introducing the use of Soundfield Systems in classrooms. With these systems, the teacher wears a radio transmitter with a microphone. The teacher's voice is sent to a radio receiver situated in the room and then amplified and relayed to the class via loudspeakers situated around the room, usually attached to the walls. These systems have been found to benefit all pupils, not just those with hearing impairment, as they are able to hear the teacher's voice more clearly. They often have the additional benefit of encouraging pupils to make less noise in the classroom and this reduction in background noise is particularly helpful to pupils with hearing impairment, with or without hearing aids. These are purchased from manufacturers, eg Connevans (details at back of booklet).

24

Hearing Aids

Hearing aids can offer a great deal of help to the majority of hearing impaired pupils. They are not often given to children with conductive hearing loss resulting from glue ear since it is a temporary loss. Occasionally a child with a conductive loss resulting from glue ear will be issued with a hearing aid, for example as a temporary measure while waiting for an operation, or if it is considered unwise to give the pupil a general anaesthetic.

Basically, hearing aids simply make sounds louder. They consist of a small microphone which collects the sound and converts it into electrical energy; an amplifier which increases the intensity of the signal; and a receiver which converts it back to sound. The system is powered by a battery. Some aids are designed to amplify some frequencies more than others (for example, mainly the higher frequencies of speech to suit a pupil with a high frequency loss, as described earlier). Individual hearing aids often have internal settings which can be altered to suit particular hearing losses. On most aids it is possible to limit the maximum output (or volume) the aid will deliver and many have a form of compression which cuts out very loud sounds that could prove uncomfortable for the wearer.

In-the-ear aids

There are different types of hearing aid available. The first type is an *in-the-ear* hearing aid, which as the name suggests fits completely in the ear canal. They are not often prescribed for young children since the outer shell of the aid will need to be replaced as the child grows and young children's ears grow very quickly. They are sometimes issued to children with an abnormal or absent pinna. They have the advantage that the microphone is situated at the usual place for picking up sound, at the ear canal, which can give a more natural sound effect. However, at present they are not suitable for profound losses as they do not give sufficient amplification.

Post-aural aids

The most common type of hearing aid issued to pupils in mainstream classes is a *post-aural* or *behind-the-ear* aid. This comprises an earmould which is made to fit the pupil and replaced as the ear grows, and the aid itself which fits behind the ear. The National Health Service (NHS) has a whole range of these aids which are identified by number (for example, BEl0l, BE36, BE55D). Many pupils with hearing impairment are adequately catered for by one of the range of NHS aids, but there is the option of a commercial hearing aid being purchased for the pupil by the NHS if this is considered necessary.

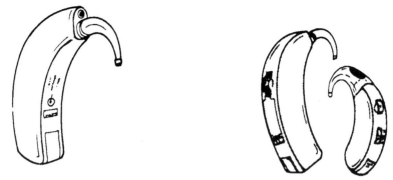

Figure 8 - Post-aural hearing aids without earmoulds.

Figure 9 - Post-aural hearing aid with earmould fitted.

Checking post-aural hearing aids

It is useful for a class teacher or special needs assistant to be able to check whether a hearing aid is functioning, as follows:

1. Check the aid visually:
    • Look at the casing to see that it is not cracked.

    • Check that the switch is working.

    • Check that the aid has a battery fitted and that it is inserted correctly.

    • Check that the earmould is not blocked with wax.

26

2. Listen to the aid:
  • Switch it on and cup the mould in the palm of your hand. It should produce a high-pitched whistle.

  • Listen via stetoclips (available from Connevans, address at back of booklet – see Figure 10). If the aid is very powerful, you may need to use an attenuator with the stetoclips (ask your visiting teacher of the deaf, or Connevans) or turn the aid down. You should get used to how speech sounds through the aid, and check that you cannot hear any distortion.

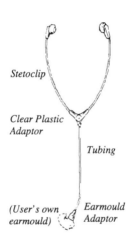

Stetoclip

Clear Plastic Adaptor

Tubing

(User's own earmould)

Earmould Adaptor

Figure 10 - Testing via a stetoclip.

3. Check again once it is fitted to the pupil:
  • Ensure that it is fitted correctly into the ear.

  • Check that it is switched on and that the volume control is correctly adjusted.

Body-worn aids
  A few children are still issued with *body-worn* hearing aids. These are very powerful aids which can give extremely high levels of amplification and can be a useful aid for a profoundly deaf child in the early stages of learning to listen and talk. With a body-worn aid, the child wears an earmould which clips onto a miniature receiver; this is in turn connected to the hearing aid by a lead. The aid itself is worn on the chest in a harness.

Figure 11 - A body-worn hearing aid.

Working with pupils wearing hearing aids
- Find out (from parents, visiting teacher of the deaf) how the aid should be set, both the switch (usually to M) and the volume.

- Check that the aid is at the correct setting, especially if the pupil does not seem to be hearing as well as usual.

- If the aid is making a high pitched whistle (feedback), check that the mould is properly fitted into the pupil's ear.

- If the mould is fitted properly but the aid still feeds back, the pupil probably needs a new mould which will entail a visit to the hospital or clinic for an impression to be taken.

- As a temporary measure, ask the pupil to reduce the volume of the aid slightly.

- Ensure that there are spare batteries available.

> • Check the aid by switching it on and turning the volume control to maximum. Then cup the mould in the palm of your hand and it should feed back. If not, fit a new battery and try again.
>
> • Listen to the aid via a stetoclip (Figure 10).

Digital hearing aids

The aids that have been described above are analogue aids. A new generation of hearing aids, digital hearing aids, has been introduced onto the market. These have the advantage that they can be adjusted more finely to suit the individual hearing impairment than acoustic hearing aids. They are likely to be increasingly prescribed for use with children. They can be tested in a similar manner to that described above for post-aural aids.

Cochlear implants

A more recent type of hearing aid, which can sometimes mistakenly be thought of as a cure for deafness, is a *cochlear implant*. A cochlear implant electrically stimulates the hearing nerve fibres directly, rather than stimulating the cochlea with amplified sound as with a conventional hearing aid. Tiny electrodes (up to 22) are surgically implanted into the cochlea, and a receiver is implanted into the mastoid bone behind the ear. The child then wears a small microphone at ear level, which sits on the pinna and looks like a post-aural aid, to collect sound, and a small transmitter which attaches to the implanted receiver by means of a magnet. Sounds are fed from the microphone to a body-worn speech processor, where they are converted into signals suitable for transmission to the receiver, which in turn passes them to the electrodes, and on to the auditory nerve and so to the brain. Figure 12 shows a cochlear implant with a body-worn speech processor as just described. Some children are now fitted with a post-aural speech processor. This sits behind the ear and looks like a post-aural hearing aid. However, it does not have an earmould and still has the magnetic coil. Children are usually switched from wearing a body-worn speech processor to a post-aural one only when they demonstrate that they are able to use the body-worn device to advantage. This is particularly true for young children as it is more difficult for a carer to monitor the functioning of the device.

Cochlear implants are used with the most profoundly deaf children who have demonstrated that they are unable to perceive sound with a conventional hearing aid. When they were first introduced they were only offered to children and adults who had gone deaf (often as a result of meningitis which damages the hair cells in the cochlea) after acquiring language. Now, however, they are increasingly being offered to children born deaf. Many people derive great benefit from their implant, although it may take two to three years or even longer for the full benefit to be realised as the wearer must learn to listen and interpret the sounds that are heard. The sounds are different from those heard by people with intact hearing. Children who have received cochlear implants are increasingly to be found in units attached to mainstream schools and mainstream classes.

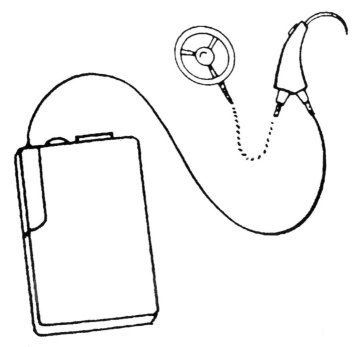

Figure 12 - A cochlear implant.

Cochlear implantation is a controversial procedure. Some members of the Deaf community are opposed to cochlear implants as they see them as a threat to their community and they also feel that the decision to go ahead with the implant should be taken by the child or young person once they have reached the age of consent, particularly since it involves a major form of surgical intervention. Unfortunately, this is not really practical since it will be too late for the child to be able to derive maximum benefit from the implant by then.

Radio hearing aids

In addition to their individual hearing aids, many hearing impaired pupils in mainstream schools are issued with radio hearing aids. These are usually used in conjunction with the pupil's own hearing aids, although some pupils are fitted with a model that incorporates a conventional body-worn hearing aid into the radio aid.

A radio aid comprises two parts: a transmitter which is worn by the teacher and which transmits the signal, and a receiver which is worn by the pupil and receives the signal.

Figure 13 - A radio aid transmitter, with microphone and aerial.

The receiver needs to be connected to the pupil's own hearing aids in order for them to hear the radio signal. The preferred method of use for most pupils is for the receiver to be connected to the pupil's individual aids by means of a lead and shoes which fit onto the aids. This is known as *direct input*. It requires that the pupil be supplied with hearing aids that have a direct input facility. Not all hearing aids in the NHS range have a direct input facility. If the pupil's aid does not have this facility, it will need to be changed. It is usually the case that the hearing aids are supplied and maintained by the NHS while the radio aids are the property of the Service for the Hearing Impaired and issued by the teacher of the deaf.

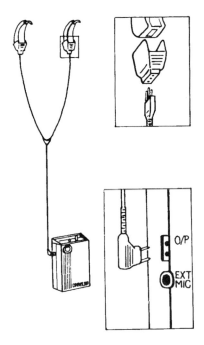

Figure 14 - A radio aid receiver with direct input lead and shoes.

The other method of using the radio aid is for the pupil to wear a loop (a circle of wire) round the neck. This is connected to the radio receiver and the signal is picked up by an induction coil in the hearing aid, which must be switched to the M/T position. If the pupil's aid does not have an M/T position, then the aid must be switched to T and an environmental microphone fitted to the receiver (as in Figure 15) in order for the pupil to hear their own voice. This is not necessary with an M/T switch. Connecting via a loop tends not to give such a good signal, although some students prefer this method since the loop can be concealed under their clothing.

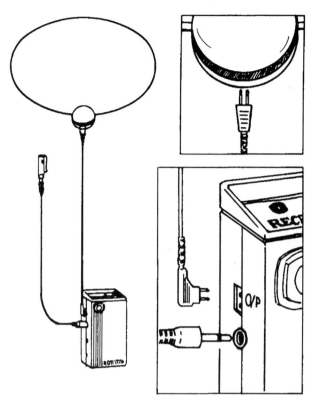

Figure 15 - A radio aid receiver with loop and environmental microphone.

Radio hearing aids make an enormous difference to a pupil's ability to discriminate speech in a mainstream classroom. While a conventional hearing aid only works well if the wearer is close to the speaker (ideally about 1–2 metres away), a radio aid operates over a long range. Radio aids therefore help to overcome the problem of distance between the pupil and teacher. They also help to reduce the effects of background noise since the microphone of the transmitter is worn close to the teacher's mouth. However, they are not a total solution and it is always beneficial to reduce both background noise and reverberation as much as possible in a classroom with a hearing aid user.

In order for the pupil to derive maximum benefit from the radio aid, the teacher needs to learn the technique of switching the transmitter on when speaking to the whole class or to a group containing the hearing impaired pupil, and switching it off when addressing a group which does not include the hearing-impaired pupil. Advice on correct use should be sought from the local Service for the Hearing Impaired. Videos are also available from the Ewing Foundation (see details at end of booklet) which help to explain both the enormous benefits of radio aids and their correct use. Connevans (address at end of booklet) have a useful booklet on all aspects of radio aid use which relates to all makes and is available free of charge on request.

Tips for using a radio hearing aid
- Position the transmitter so that the microphone is 10–15 centimetres from your mouth.

- Always switch it on when addressing the whole class or a group containing the pupil wearing a radio aid.

- Switch the transmitter off when talking to a group that does not contain the radio aid wearer.

- Always switch off at break times etc. (otherwise the pupil may hear something you would rather they did not).

- If possible, connect the transmitter to audio or video equipment if using a cassette or video in class (seek advice from the Service for the Hearing Impaired).

- Still keep in mind the necessity for providing good listening conditions and good conditions for lip-reading.

Wearing a radio transmitter and switching it on and off appropriately should not be onerous for a teacher. There are usually alternative ways of wearing the transmitter, for example it can hang round the neck from a neck harness, or be worn at the waist or in a jacket pocket with a satellite microphone in a similar way to that in which television presenters wear their transmitters. Occasionally a teacher may not use the transmitter appropriately, for example by leaving it on the desk, or may refuse to wear it. This case is discussed in the *Disability Discrimination Act Code of Practice for Schools* and the conclusion is drawn that if a teacher were to refuse to use the radio microphone it is likely that this would be unlawful.

Difficulties with hearing aids

In addition to a loss of hearing, some pupils experience other hearing difficulties. Some hearing impaired pupils have a very limited dynamic range of hearing. This means that they cannot hear a sound until it is a certain intensity, but then when it is turned up a little more, it becomes unbearably loud. A hearing aid can be adjusted to account for this problem. It may not be readily apparent when the hearing aid is fitted in the clinic, but obvious in the class setting. A teacher noticing that a pupil wearing hearing aids finds loud noises cause discomfort should report this fact to the pupil's parents or the visiting teacher of the deaf, as it may be that the pupil is suffering discomfort and compensating by turning the aid down, which means that they will not hear conversation clearly.

It is also possible to turn up a hearing aid beyond its peak performance with the result that sound becomes distorted. For this reason it is important that any hearing aid, radio aid or other amplifying equipment used by hearing impaired pupils should be precisely set for the individual and the teacher made aware of the correct settings.

Possible causes for rejection of hearing aids
- The aid is uncomfortable (may need a new earmould, replacement of tubing or a different aid).

- Loud noises are causing discomfort (aid may need to have internal settings changed, or different aid prescribed).

- The pupil may not have accepted the need for an aid, or may be going through a difficult phase (individual counselling can help).

- The pupil may be experiencing teasing by other pupils (this can be difficult to uncover, especially if the pupil is normally quiet).

- The pupil may feel isolated if he or she is the only pupil in a mainstream school with hearing aids (explore possibilities for meeting other pupils with hearing aids).

It is also possible for pupils to reject radio hearing aids, particularly if they are the only one in a school fitted with one.

Possible causes for rejecting radio hearing aids
- It may not be adjusted properly (all radio aids should be set by a qualified teacher of the deaf or audiologist).

- The pupil may be being teased (often an explanation and demonstration of how the aid works increases understanding and reduces teasing).

- The pupil may feel embarrassed by wearing it (there may be a way of wearing it that makes it less conspicuous).

- The pupil may feel that the teacher regards wearing the transmitter as a nuisance (staff INSET on the benefits of radio aids can help – videos from the Ewing Foundation, listed at the back of the booklet, are designed to help with this problem).

The Effects of Hearing Impairment

The effects of a hearing loss are not always straightforward or easy to identify. For the mainstream teacher there are several possible indicators of hearing loss to be aware of.

Possible indicators of hearing loss
- A history of ear infections, catarrh, runny nose;

- failure to respond immediately to instructions;

- instances of mishearing;

- paying close attention to the speaker's face in order to lip-read;

- speech problems;

- difficulty with phonics;

- turning the head to one side (this can indicate a loss in one ear);

- inattentiveness.

These may not, of course, be symptoms of a hearing loss, but they are worth following up, particularly in a child with a history of early hearing difficulties. (See Webster and Wood, 1989, for greater discussion of this point.)

The effects of a hearing impairment can permeate all aspects of the curriculum and lead to both generalised learning difficulties and difficulties in specific areas. There are several possible major areas of difficulty: the first is either not hearing or hearing only part of what has been said, thus leading to misunderstanding. This has been explained in the previous chapters.

The second problem relates to the delay in language acquisition which often (although not always) accompanies a hearing impairment. Particularly in pupils with mild or moderate hearing losses, the effects can be difficult to detect. The pupil may appear to have understood and may well think that they have understood, but on closer examination they have either misunderstood or only partially understood. There may be gaps in the pupil's vocabulary, which have resulted partly from the generalised language delay and partly from them not overhearing to the extent that children with normal hearing do. Children with normal hearing learn some of their vocabulary from overhearing the conversation of adults.

Pupils with hearing impairment frequently know only one meaning for a word that has several meanings, which can lead to real misunderstandings. For example, they may know the literal meaning of the word 'jump', but metaphorical meanings such as 'jump through hoops' may well evade them. While it could be argued that pupils with learning difficulties not resulting from hearing impairment have similar problems, the difference is that in pupils whose difficulties arise as a result of hearing impairment such lack of knowledge may be unexpected and therefore go undetected.

In addition, they may have an inadequate grasp of concepts. However, once they have grasped an idea, they are able to move ahead at the same rate as their normally hearing peers.

Another possible cause of learning difficulty is that pupils with hearing impairment may have more limited experience of life than their normally hearing peers. This can happen quite inadvertently as parents and carers either behave in a more protective manner towards children with hearing impairment, aware that they may not hear warning signs of danger such as traffic noise, or they limit their experience by not asking them to take messages or visit shops on account of their delayed language acquisition. This can lead to both a lack of experience and an attitude in the pupil with hearing impairment that is more dependent on the adults around them. This in turn can influence their learning style in school.

Reading

Many pupils with hearing impairment experience difficulties with reading. There are several possible sources of difficulty. Firstly, if the pupil has delayed language acquisition then it may well be the case that the language of the reading material is beyond their level of spoken language development. Children usually learn to read after they have learnt to talk, but for hearing impaired pupils the process of learning to read may need to progress alongside language acquisition. Webster (1986) describes these difficulties and the strategies that pupils with hearing impairment may develop.

Pupils with hearing impairment have shown different responses to the introduction of the Literacy Strategy. Many have responded positively and have benefited from the structure and style of presentation. In the past, teachers have frequently shied away from teaching reading to pupils with hearing impairment using phonics, on the grounds that the pupils will not be able to hear the individual sounds clearly. The demands of the Literacy Strategy and the Literacy Hour have meant that pupils with hearing impairment are increasingly included with their peers and subject to the same expectations. Provided that there are good listening conditions and any appropriate technical aids are used (pupil's individual hearing aids; radio aid; soundfield system etc.) many pupils with hearing impairment have demonstrated that they are able to use phonics. The requirement for good listening conditions may mean that pupils with hearing impairment fare better if they can be withdrawn to a quiet room or area of the classroom. Although this may not be the usual practice, this is one situation when withdrawal for at least part of the Hour may be justified. The RNID Education Guidelines publication *Promoting Literacy in Deaf Pupils* listed at the back of the booklet contains many practical suggestions for promoting literacy development in pupils with hearing impairment.

Personal and social development

There are steps that can be taken to facilitate the personal and social development of pupils with hearing impairment. The school should make provision for meeting the needs of pupils with hearing impairment and, under the terms of the *Disability Discrimination Act*, could be found guilty of discrimination if they have failed to do so. Since conductive hearing loss is so prevalent in young children, primary schools should anticipate that they will have pupils with hearing impairment and ensure that all staff have some general awareness of how to cater for their needs. This could address such topics as:

- conversing with pupils with hearing impairment;

- checking that the pupil has understood instructions;

- providing a written version of verbal instructions, eg for homework;

- ensuring that the pupil is included;

- providing breaks from continuous listening;

- giving opportunities for pupils with hearing impairment to take the lead and exercise their strengths.

When pupils feel genuinely included and appropriate allowances are made for their hearing impairment they are less likely to encounter social and emotional difficulties. If difficulties do arise, it is important to try to uncover their source. If the child's speech is unclear or their language is delayed they may find it difficult to communicate meaningfully with other pupils and become frustrated, eventually possibly giving vent to their frustration in ways that are unacceptable. It may be that the child with hearing impairment is being teased or bullied or left out of games. One reason for a child being excluded from games can be that they do not understand the rules, which may even change frequently. Another pupil may be encouraged to undertake to explain the rules, or occasionally the whole class could engage in a game in PE that could be played in the playground. It is easy for pupils who are unable to hear clearly to feel left out of conversations or jokes or to think that others are talking about them. Again, other pupils can help by taking positive steps to include pupils with hearing impairment. While it may seem tedious at first to repeat a joke, if it is retold well then the others will probably enjoy hearing it again.

As pupils mature, they need to form a clear concept of their own identity. While this is true for all pupils, for those with hearing impairment there is another layer of complexity. They will be faced with such questions as: How do they view themselves? Do they see themselves as fitting in with hearing society, or are they more comfortable with others with hearing impairment? If the latter is true, then do they identify with the Deaf community and wish to embrace its language and culture? Pupils who have cochlear implants may feel a close affinity with others who have cochlear implants and see their identity as part of a distinct group. It is possible for pupils with hearing impairment, as with any pupil, to see themselves as having several different identities and to move happily between them. Difficulties can sometimes arise when pupils with hearing impairment see themselves as not fitting with either the hearing community or the Deaf community and end up feeling isolated. Where a pupil is the only member of their family with a hearing impairment and possibly the only pupil in their class or school with a significant hearing impairment they may feel a strong sense of isolation and lack of belonging. This does not hold true for all pupils with hearing impairment, many of whom do not suffer problems of identity or adjustment, but the possibility of such feelings should be borne in mind and if necessary counselling should be offered.

Behavioural difficulties

Behavioural difficulties can arise from inappropriate management of pupils with hearing impairment. Under the terms of the *Disability Discrimination Act*, all staff dealing with pupils with hearing impairment should receive training in how to communicate with them. There are several general guidelines that should be followed, as summarised in the table below.

Conversing with pupils with hearing impairment
- Gain the pupils' attention before speaking.

- Make sure they can see your face.

- Speak clearly, but do not exaggerate your lip patterns.

- Ensure that the light is falling on your face.

- Try not to walk about too much.

- Ensure that hearing aids are worn at all times.

- Use radio aids when appropriate.

- Make sure they understand the subject of the conversation.

- If they have not understood, rephrase using different words rather than repeating a phrase several times.

- Meaningful gestures can aid understanding.

- Make sure they are included in the conversation.

- When possible repeat what other pupils have said (wrong answers as well as correct ones).

- Reduce background noise.

- Make good use of visual clues (eg pictures) and write new vocabulary on the board.

With respect to managing pupils with hearing impairment, it is essential that basic communication techniques are followed such as ensuring that pupils have understood instructions and explanations. What may be perceived as inappropriate behaviour may result from a failure of communication. For example a pupil with hearing impairment may continue with an activity after being told to stop. Particularly in difficult listening conditions, such as in a school hall or gym, it is quite possible that the pupil did not hear the instruction to stop. While it is appropriate to expect the same standard of behaviour from pupils with hearing impairment, it is also vital to make the necessary allowance for difficulties in hearing or lack of understanding. If a pupil with hearing impairment is punished for behaviour when adequate attention has not been given to that pupil's difficulties in hearing and communication, the school could be guilty of discrimination.

The effort involved in concentrating for long periods in order to understand, often by listening attentively and watching closely in order to lip-read, can be very tiring. It is important that pupils with hearing impairment are given frequent breaks from work requiring such high levels of concentration. If pupils with hearing impairment are put under too much strain, especially if they are finding it difficult to understand the work, they sometimes exhibit unacceptable behaviour as a result of the frustration of the situation. While the behaviour is unacceptable, the reasons behind it should be understood and often the best way of dealing with the behavioural difficulty is by changing the situation in some way.

It is important that the strengths of pupils with hearing impairment are recognised and built upon. They should be given the opportunity to lead as well as to follow, and to assist other pupils. Their individual skills should be discovered and developed.

Communication

There are different communication approaches used with pupils with hearing impairment. The majority of pupils with hearing impairment in mainstream settings will use spoken language as their main means of communication, whatever their degree of hearing impairment. Suggestions made so far in relation to the provision of good listening conditions; use of hearing aids, radio aids or soundfield systems; ensuring pupils have the opportunity to lip-read; the use of additional visual support in terms of pictures or key vocabulary are all intended to aid access to spoken language. The suggestions regarding how to converse with pupils with hearing impairment, the importance of checking their understanding and rephrasing if they have not understood will assist when teaching pupils whose language development may be delayed as a result of their hearing impairment. This type of communication approach is referred to as an *oral approach*, or *aural-oral approach*. Other terms used are *natural aural approach* or *auditory verbal*. There are some differences in these various oral approaches but they all involve the use of spoken language supported by appropriate technological aids to listening. Pupils with cochlear implants are increasingly being educated using an oral approach, despite their profound degree of hearing impairment.

Total communication

The term 'total communication' is used to cover a range of situations and communication approaches. In its original use, it referred to a philosophy that suggested the use of whatever strategies would facilitate communication with an individual. This could include spoken language; lip-reading; gesture; sign; hearing etc. So a resource base for pupils with hearing impairment might describe its philosophy as 'total communication' and mean that different communication approaches are used according to the needs of individual pupils. However, it is often used to describe a communication approach in which spoken language is used together with hearing aids if appropriate and key words are signed at the same time. The signs are borrowed from British Sign Language (BSL) and used in conjunction with speech. The pupil is expected to extract meaning from the simultaneous presentation of speech and signs.

Bilingualism

A minority of pupils with hearing impairment are taught using a bilingual approach. The two languages used will be BSL and either spoken or written English. In order to distinguish it from other forms of bilingualism that use two spoken languages, it may be referred to as sign bilingualism. A sign language such as BSL is a language in its own right, with its own structure and syntax. It is not possible to speak and sign at the same time since the word order of spoken language and the order of the signs is different. Pupils using a sign bilingual approach will need to have lessons presented to them in BSL. They may be taught as part of a mainstream class with the material signed to them by an interpreter, a teacher of the deaf, a communication support worker or learning support assistant. For many pupils in a sign bilingual approach, BSL is their first or preferred language, with English in its spoken or written form as a second language. Pupils whose home language is another spoken language will need to be multilingual. Some pupils in a bilingual approach will decide not to use hearing aids, while others will use them for at least part of the day.

The emphasis of this booklet is on supporting pupils who are being educated in a mainstream setting using an oral approach. It is anticipated that pupils using total communication or a sign bilingual approach will have a Statement of Special Educational Need and be supported by external agencies or by teachers of the deaf on site and that particular advice concerning their communication needs will be offered on an individual basis.

Responding to Educational Needs

The introduction of the *Special Educational Needs Code of Practice* in 1994 provided a framework for assessing and responding to the needs of pupils with SEN including pupils with hearing impairment. The revised *Code of Practice* introduced in 2002 simplified the process to some extent, but the introduction of the *Code of Practice for Schools* in relation to the *Disability Discrimination Act* places additional responsibilities on schools. Since these documents are central to assessing and meeting the needs of pupils with SEN, some knowledge of these two codes is assumed.

Early Years Action or School Action
The *Special Educational Needs Code of Practice* envisages a 'graduated response' to provide individual help to pupils with SEN. Where action is taken that is additional to or different from that provided for other pupils, this is defined as Early Years Action or School Action depending on the educational setting. There are some strategies that are likely to help many pupils with hearing impairment, including those with conductive hearing loss and unilateral hearing loss discussed earlier. Here is a summary:

Helping pupils with hearing impairment
- Ensure that the pupil is paying visual attention before commencing, if necessary by saying the pupil's name.

- Check that the pupil has understood instructions (this is best done discreetly).

- Encourage the pupil to check if they have not heard fully, by asking you or another pupil.

- Whenever possible give visual clues, by writing page numbers on the board/projector; use pictures to help with new vocabulary; use examples to explain words that are not immediately clear.

- Ensure that you are not standing with your back to the window and that the room has sufficient light.

- Reduce background noise in the classroom.

These strategies could be a topic for INSET for all staff, provided by a specialist teacher of the deaf. Additional ideas can be found in the RNID publication *Guidelines for mainstream teachers with deaf pupils in their class* (2000).

One helpful approach to identification is to draw up a checklist of possible difficulties for pupils with mild to moderate hearing problems and tick those that apply to the pupil in question. Possible indicators of hearing impairment were discussed in the chapter Understanding Hearing Loss, with particular reference to pupils with mild and moderate losses who are likely to be helped under Early Years Action or School Action. A checklist could include the following:

- difficulty in following instructions;

- difficulty in hearing at close range unless teacher raises their voice;

- difficulty in hearing across the room;

- short concentration span;

- inability to follow a story;

- limited vocabulary;

- immature speech (articulation) or language;

- frequently asking for repetition of instructions;

- withdrawn behaviour;

- appearing to hear better at one side of the room than the other;

- speaking loudly (or very quietly).

While some of these factors can also be indicators of other difficulties, they are frequently associated with hearing difficulties.

The needs of individual pupils with hearing impairment can vary greatly. For pupils with hearing impairment who are being provided with intervention as part of Early Years Action or School Action, it is important for the school to gain information regarding the pupils' hearing impairment from parents and if possible from other sources. Parents should be aware of any history of hearing loss and be able to supply the vital information concerning the pupil's current hearing status and whether treatment has been initiated or is continuing, and also any strategies that they have adopted at home which they have found beneficial. It is also useful to observe parents interacting with the pupil as this can reveal strategies of which they may be unaware themselves, for example they may always touch the child to gain attention before speaking.

The pupil's own opinion can be enlightening. They often know the best seating position for them in class, or the situations in which they find it difficult to hear. This may reveal an unhelpful habit on the part of the teacher, for example in dropping their voice at the end of a sentence or standing with their back to the window when addressing the class, making lip-reading virtually impossible. It may also offer some explanation concerning the pupil's perceived behavioural difficulties, for example the pupil may not be able to hear in the poorer acoustic conditions of the hall and therefore not immediately follow instructions in PE.

While it is anticipated that intervention will be provided from the school's own resources, a one-off assessment from an external source, for example a visiting teacher of the deaf, can provide ideas on strategies or equipment that might be useful. A visiting teacher of the deaf can also explore the pupil's ability to discriminate speech in different settings or at different distances. Once a pupil's needs have been defined, an Individual Education Plan (IEP) is drawn up to specify the intervention that is planned. Many of these pupils are likely to have a fluctuating conductive hearing impairment or a mild or moderate permanent loss. Precise targets will need to be set for each pupil. They are likely to centre on:

- making appropriate adjustments to the learning environment to enable the pupil to make maximum use of their hearing;

- providing a quiet area where the pupil can concentrate more easily;

- encouraging the development of listening skills and/or encouraging the use of alternative strategies, for example recognising visual patterns in spelling;

- checking that the pupil has understood;

- giving the pupil the opportunity to work as a member of a small group;

- creating many opportunities for the pupil to experience success to increase confidence;

- specific work on language development;

- support with reading and writing.

Making appropriate adjustments to the learning environment to enable maximum use of hearing

This may involve moving the whole class to a quieter room, or one that is not open plan. Consideration should be given to the provision of curtains and carpets and acoustic treatment of the room, which may include such major steps as fitting a false ceiling. The teacher should consider their own teaching style: do they encourage pupils to keep the level of noise in the room to a working 'hum', or do they tolerate high levels of background noise? If the teacher tends to address the class from their table, is this situated in a position such that it is easy for all pupils to see their face, with the light falling on it?

Are any pupils with known hearing loss seated in an advantageous position, as outlined earlier? Is this the case not only in the classroom, but also in any other room where the pupils are taught? Has consideration been given to the nature of the hearing loss, with appropriate arrangements made for pupils with unilateral hearing loss, or wearing hearing aids? These points were discussed earlier.

Providing a quiet area where the pupil can concentrate more easily

A quiet area of the room in which to work can greatly assist the concentration of pupils with hearing impairment. While the trend to offer support to pupils in the classroom rather than withdrawing them is generally successful, particular consideration needs to be given to the needs of pupils with hearing impairment. It may be so much easier for them to hear that they choose to do some of their work in a quiet area.

Encouraging the development of listening skills and/or encouraging alternative strategies

The emphasis of the booklet has been on encouraging pupils to make the maximum use of their hearing and to develop listening skills. The use of listening games and focused listening activities can be very helpful. These may need to be at a simple level to begin with, for example involving large differences like those between a word with one syllable compared to a word with three syllables. Commercial games, such as sound lotto, are useful with some pupils, but others may find these too difficult initially and it may be preferable for them to make their own listening game by going round the school and recording different sounds.

Where listening is difficult, pupils should be helped to use visual patterns as well. Their attention can be drawn to visual patterns in spelling. Some pupils with hearing impairment have a good eye for detail and remember visual patterns well. Attention can be drawn to different lip patterns, but it is very important not to distort the way one speaks in the process as this can destroy both the pattern itself and the rhythm of speech, thus making things more difficult.

Checking that the pupil has understood

This is vital. Earlier chapters have detailed the reasons why pupils with hearing impairment may not understand – because either they have not heard or the language or vocabulary is beyond their grasp. Checking understanding should be done discreetly. Asking directly whether a pupil has understood is likely to elicit the answer yes, especially if they are eager to please.

Where understanding has not taken place, it is a good idea to break instructions down into smaller steps. A pupil with hearing impairment may have difficulty in retaining three instructions, but be able to respond to one at a time. Sometimes a friend will act as a 'buddy' to a pupil with hearing impairment. This can be very helpful so long as it is not taken too far.

Giving the pupil the opportunity to work as a member of a group

Pupils with hearing impairment benefit from working in a variety of settings and situations. They may benefit from individual support and work in small groups with similar difficulties, but they are also likely to benefit from being part of a small group. This can increase their confidence if they are able to hear and be heard easily and they may feel happier contributing in a small group. They should be given the same opportunities as other pupils to take the lead, and any attempt on the part of other pupils to dominate them should be discouraged.

Creating opportunities for the pupil to experience success

It can be easy to overlook the strengths of a pupil who has a hearing impairment. Their difficulties and need for support may be obvious, and it can be more difficult to uncover their strengths, particularly if the pupil is rather quiet. It can be tempting not to make them the leader in any situation as they may not immediately grasp instructions, but this tendency should be resisted.

Specific work on language development

As part of the assessment, it may become clear that the pupil with hearing impairment has associated language difficulties. These difficulties may relate to language in general, or to specific areas such as vocabulary. Possible areas of weakness are outlined in the section The Effects of Hearing Impairment. Once these have been uncovered, then some targeted work can be implemented. For example, work on vocabulary could include not just checking that a pupil knows certain items of vocabulary, but getting them to suggest alternative words, or seeing how many words they can think of to describe something that is big.

If there is a general delay in language, then engaging the pupil in conversation will encourage development. Giving extra time and attention to talking things through will help the pupil with hearing impairment to express themselves. It is important to give them extra time to think, as it can take longer for them to process what they have heard and formulate a reply. Teachers should beware of slipping into the habit of asking too many questions, especially closed questions (yes/no type) or those that require only a single word response. It is better to be less controlling, to ask fewer questions and encourage pupils with hearing impairment to express their ideas themselves.

Support with reading and writing

This is vital for pupils with hearing impairment. The Effects of Hearing Impairment above details some of the potential difficulties related to learning to read. In the early stages, a paired or shared reading approach is likely to prove beneficial. Reading work can be based on sharing books, with the pupil joining in as they feel able. Readers wishing to pursue the topic in more detail are referred to Webster (1986) or Wood (1986).

Writing can also present difficulties for a pupil with hearing impairment. If their own language is delayed, then it is not surprising if they have difficulty with written language. A developmental or emergent approach to writing in the early stages has proved helpful with some pupils with hearing impairment. It is important that teachers do not expect a pupil with hearing impairment and associated language delay to produce written work which is in advance of their spoken language. It may be easier for the pupil to dictate to an adult.

For further suggestions on support with literacy, see the RNID publication *Promoting literacy in deaf pupils,* details of which can be found at the back of this booklet.

Reviewing IEPs

The progress of pupils with hearing impairment who are being offered intervention under Early Years Action or School Action should be kept under constant review. The IEPs should be reviewed at least three times a year, seeking the opinion of parents on the pupil's progress.

Figure 16 is an example of an IEP for a pupil in Year 2 with a history of conductive hearing loss, whose hearing is currently within normal limits. It seeks to encourage a rapid improvement in her concentration and sets precise targets for reading and writing. A learning support assistant is to be used to support the targets by promoting listening skills and letter-sound correspondence under the direction of the class teacher.

The use of a learning support assistant can be extremely beneficial, but it requires planning on the part of the class teacher. The assistant should not be expected to work without direction, nor to take responsibility for the pupil's learning. They will usually work in the context of the classroom. However, as mentioned earlier in this section, some pupils with hearing impairment find it less stressful to work in a quiet room. Focused listening work such as that suggested in this IEP may be best undertaken in a quiet area of the classroom or in a separate room.

Name: Theresa Brown   **DOB:** 27.10.1995   **Year:** Y2   **Age:** 7y 0m

Nature of concerns: Theresa has difficulty in concentrating in class. She frequently fails to hear instructions accurately. Her speech contains some immaturities and her vocabulary is limited. She has made slow progress with reading, depending largely on context clues. Her spelling shows little evidence of use of sound-letter correspondence.

Assessment: Reading NC level 1; Spelling level 1. English Picture Vocabulary Test age equivalent level 5 years 6 months.

Background information: Theresa has been attending the audiology clinic from age 4. She recently had an operation for the insertion of grommets and her hearing at the most recent test was within normal limits. Her hearing will continue to be monitored regularly at the audiology clinic.

She was assessed by the speech and language therapist and the report indicated a moderate delay in language development and some phonological substitutions. The speech and language therapist suggested a programme to be carried out by Theresa's parents and continued in school.

Action:
- Continue to provide sympathetic listening conditions in class, with small group work and the opportunity for Theresa to work in a quiet area of the classroom.

- Provide daily 15-minute session with classroom assistant working on promoting listening skills using worksheets from classroom, and on letter-sound correspondence.

- Monitor progress during the Literacy Hour.

- Provide opportunities for Theresa to take the lead in some small group work.

- Encourage her parents to take Theresa to their local library and to read with her using 'paired reading' scheme as adopted in school generally. In particular parents to be encouraged to prompt Theresa to attempt the initial sound of unfamiliar words.

Targets to be achieved by review:
- Theresa to be able to recognise all individual consonants in initial position and some familiar blends (sh, sl, br, bl, ch).

- To be able to select either the correct word from the Breakthrough word bank or consistently to select one with the correct initial letter sound.

- To be able to select the correct onset for words beginning with individual consonants or blends as listed above and to be able to change these to create different words with the same rime.

Date for review: 6 months

Figure 16 - An Individual Education Plan.

Early Years Action Plus or School Action Plus

The next level of intervention is entitled Early Years Action Plus or School Action Plus. Intervention at this level is characterised by the involvement of external support services. In the case of pupils with hearing impairment, the local visiting teacher of the deaf is likely to be requested to assess the pupil and offer advice or direct teaching. With respect to individual pupils, the teacher of the deaf would be expected to contribute to the setting of new targets for their IEP. A pupil could be included under Early Years Action Plus or School Action Plus if they continue to fail to make adequate progress despite the intervention offered under the Early Years Action or the School Action arrangements, or pupils with hearing impairment could be included at this level immediately if they require 'specialist equipment or regular advice or visits by a specialist service' (*Code of Practice* p.55). Some pupils are likely to be included at this level who would previously have been the subject of a Statement of Special Educational Need.

The involvement of the teacher of the deaf need not be restricted to the individual pupil with hearing impairment, but could take the form of more generalised advice on management strategies that would benefit other pupils in addition to those with hearing impairment. The precise nature of the support or intervention offered will vary from one Service for the Hearing Impaired to another, according to local agreements. Teachers of the deaf from some Services will offer direct support to pupils, while those attached to another Service will offer advice but not direct support. In some cases, the teacher of the deaf may be called in to offer advice for one pupil and then deliver INSET for all staff that will assist the school in meeting the requirements of the Disability Discrimination Act. The nature of the support or intervention from the teacher of the deaf may include:

- assessment of individual pupils, including language development; literacy; ability to discriminate speech in different settings;

- audit of the school's acoustic conditions;

- advice on appropriate technical equipment for the individual pupil, eg a radio aid, or for the school, eg a soundfield system for the classroom;

- advice on modifications for assessments;

- input into the planning and review of IEPs;

- regular monitoring of progress and advice to staff;

- direct individual teaching for pupils with hearing impairment;

- INSET for staff;

- Deaf Awareness sessions for staff and pupils.

In some areas a Service Agreement will be drawn up between the Service for the Hearing Impaired and the school. This will detail what the Service will provide and what the school will provide.

Where individual support is provided for a hearing impaired pupil this can take the form of in-class support or be offered on a withdrawal basis. The decision concerning where and how this support is offered is a vital one. There can be distinct advantages for a hearing impaired pupil in support being given outside the classroom. This can open up the possibility of working in a quiet area, which provides a much improved listening environment for the pupil. Some pupils who wear hearing aids actively seek opportunities of working in a withdrawal situation for this reason, claiming that listening in the mainstream class setting for long periods is stressful. Additionally, if the support being offered is concentrating on a different area from the rest of the group or is presenting work in advance which is to be presented to the whole group, then it may be appropriate for such help to be offered in another room.

However, there are some hearing impaired pupils who actively resent being withdrawn from class at all, and their wishes need to be considered. In any case, it must be quite clear if a pupil is being withdrawn that the support that they are being offered on a one-to-one basis is highly relevant and is not resulting in them missing out on other work.

Some pupils resent the presence of another adult in the room offering them in-class support so this situation needs to be handled very sensitively. A support teacher can often be used in a team teaching role, but this would clearly not be appropriate for a learning support assistant. A decision needs to be made concerning the positioning of the learning support assistant. If the role of the assistant is to act as note-taker for the pupil then it is probably preferable for the assistant to sit at the back of the class and be as inconspicuous as possible. However, sometimes a learning support assistant or support teacher is provided in order to assist the pupil in accessing the curriculum and is expected to explain unfamiliar vocabulary or difficult linguistic concepts. This demands not only skill on the part of the adult but also a great deal of sensitivity in order to ensure that they are not offering too much help and removing the necessity from the pupil to work things out for themselves. The effective use of additional help in the classroom can be a difficult area (Thomas, 1992).

Thus the question of the support offered to pupils must be given very careful consideration. The visiting teacher of the hearing impaired should be able to offer advice tailored to the individual pupil's needs and the school setting.

Statements of Special Educational Needs

Pupils with hearing impairment may be referred for statutory assessment leading to a Statement of Special Educational Need. There are variations between LEAs regarding criteria for assessment for a Statement or regarding a decision on whether to draw up a Statement. Some pupils with hearing impairment will be referred for statutory assessment prior to school entry. It is assumed that those pupils who require sign support or who are being educated using a sign bilingual approach will either be the subject of a Statement or will be educated in a resource base that offers support for the approach. In either case, it is assumed that specific advice will be available concerning that pupil's communication needs and how these are to be met locally.

A Whole School Policy

Under the *Code of Practice*, each school should have in place a policy outlining their provision for pupils with special educational needs. As part of this policy, consideration should be given to the assessment and arrangements made for pupils with hearing difficulties.

For any class of pupils entering school in Reception, there is an expectation that a sizeable minority of pupils will have a fluctuating hearing loss (Webster and Wood, 1989). If parents are asked to complete a form detailing any difficulties their child has, then a specific question should be included relating to history of frequent colds or ear infections. The names of these pupils should be given to the class teacher so that they are aware of possible difficulties.

Consideration can be given to providing any pupils on this list (and others considered in need of it) with short sessions of small group work targeted on listening skills, early phonic work, or work related to reading and spelling. This could easily be undertaken by a classroom assistant under the guidance of the class teacher and would be aimed at preventing difficulties or picking them up early.

All staff in a first or infant school, including secretaries and lunch-time supervisors, would benefit from a session of INSET related to raising awareness of hearing loss and strategies for helping. This could result in improved management of pupils' behaviour since pupils who are not hearing properly may be more inclined to misbehave. Some strategies could be suggested in the INSET for inclusion in the school's behaviour policy, for example encouraging pupils to reduce background noise in the classroom.

A whole school approach to supporting pupils with hearing impairment in the first school
- Always gain the pupils' attention before speaking.

- Look at them when talking to them.

- Speak clearly but do not exaggerate lip patterns or shout.

- Do not expect them to hear from a distance.

- Use gestures to help understanding.

- Remember it is very difficult to hear outside.

- Ensure hearing aids and radio aids are used if supplied.

- Pay extra attention to road safety.

- Do not over-protect them.

- Allow them to experience success.

The headteacher may choose to designate some classroom assistant time to working with pupils with hearing difficulties. A single session of INSET would be unlikely to be of sufficient benefit to offer adequate advice or suggestions, but many Services for Hearing Impaired Pupils offer courses for classroom assistants. While these are often aimed specifically at those working with pupils with severe losses, they may prove very beneficial for assistants working regularly with pupils with less severe losses, helping them to develop expertise in the area. There is clearly a cost implication here, but this may well help to prevent some pupils from experiencing difficulties later.

Where a school has a pupil or pupils with severe or profound hearing losses on roll, then some INSET for all staff is vital. This may only need to be a short session for most staff who are not directly involved, while others will clearly need more help. Hearing pupils will benefit from Deaf Awareness training to help them in relating to the hearing impaired pupils. Aspects of hearing loss and its implications can usefully be built into many strands of the National Curriculum.

By the time they reach secondary school, those pupils who suffered from conductive hearing loss resulting from ear infections and glue ear are likely to have grown out of their hearing difficulties. However, they may sometimes be left with listening difficulties or resulting learning difficulties. Information concerning the pupil's medical history can help staff to understand their present problems. A policy that includes some means of ensuring that relevant information of this kind is passed on to all staff will therefore be beneficial.

Parents

Parents of pupils with hearing difficulties are usually well aware of their problems with hearing and often also of the associated learning difficulties. For those pupils with conductive hearing losses which require monitoring and medical or surgical treatment, it is vital that there is close liaison between home and school so that the teacher is aware of the pupil's current hearing status and of any planned intervention. For all parents of pupils with hearing impairment, co-operation between home and school is vital. In some areas, the Service for the Hearing Impaired takes main responsibility for liaison with parents of pupils with more severe losses. It is likely that members of the Service will have been in touch with such families since the child was very young, and in some cases the teacher of the deaf will be the Key Worker under the *Children Act.*

Some parents of pupils with sensori-neural losses may need help in coming to terms both with the existence of the hearing loss and the fact that it is permanent. This scenario will be a familiar one to teachers of the hearing impaired, but for pupils where the loss is mild or high frequency in nature the loss may have only been discovered shortly before school entry and the peripatetic teacher of the hearing impaired may not have become very involved with the family.

If a class teacher or SENCO becomes aware that parents are under the impression that a pupil will grow out of a hearing loss which reports suggest is permanent, then it is advisable to involve another professional who is seen as having some expert knowledge in the field. The school nurse may be the most helpful, especially if she is already known to the family. Alternatively the advisory teacher of the hearing impaired can be consulted for advice even if the pupil is not at Early Years Action Plus or School Action Plus of the *Code of Practice.* It is usually the case that the Service for the Hearing Impaired is closely involved with the local audiology service and ENT consultants and in a position to get the question raised at the pupil's next appointment.

Many pupils with severe and profound hearing losses are now integrated into mainstream classes. Parents may see the class teacher more regularly than the specialist teacher so the class teacher can be more aware of parents' anxieties. It can sometimes be distressing for parents of pupils with hearing impairment if they suddenly become aware of the implications of the hearing loss in some new way. This sometimes happens at a school concert if the parents of a pupil with hearing impairment realise that their child is not singing in time with the other pupils or is singing out of tune. Sensitivity on the part of the class teacher towards parents' feelings and responses can be invaluable in easing the situation.

The increase in integration of hearing impaired pupils into mainstream classes has meant that many more mainstream teachers are now encountering pupils with all degrees of hearing impairment in their classes. While this can prove to be a challenge for mainstream teachers and pupils with hearing impairment alike, many hearing impaired pupils are very successfully integrated. Mainstream staff who have equipped themselves with some basic understanding of hearing impairment and possible strategies for intervention are likely to be in a better position to make the integration of these pupils successful.

The final point that should have become clear by this stage is that successful provision for pupils with hearing difficulties, be they associated with a mild conductive loss or a severe sensori-neural loss, involves the active co-operation of all those involved with the pupils, parents and professionals alike.

References and Further Reading

Bamford, J and Saunders, E (1991) *Hearing Impairment, Auditory Perception and Language Disability* (Second Edition). London: Whurr.

Beveridge, S (1996) *Spotlight on Special Educational Needs: Learning Difficulties*. Tamworth: NASEN.

DfES (2001) *Special Educational Needs Code of Practice*. London: DfES.

Lynas, W (1986) *Integrating the Handicapped into Ordinary Schools – A Study of Hearing Impaired Pupils*. Beckenham, Kent: Croom Helm.

Nolan, M and Tucker, I (1988) *The Hearing Impaired Child and the Family* (New Edition). London: Souvenir Press, Human Horizons Series.

Reed, M (1984) *Educating Hearing Impaired Children*. Open University Press.

RNID (2000) *Guidelines for mainstream teachers with deaf pupils in their class*. London: RNID.

RNID (2001) *Promoting literacy in deaf pupils*. London: RNID.

Thomas, G (1992) *Effective Classroom Teamwork: support or intrusion?* London: Routledge.

Tucker, I and Powell, C (1991) *The Hearing Impaired Child and School*. London. Souvenir Press, Human Horizons Series.

Watson, L, Gregory, S and Powers, S (1999) *Deaf and Hearing Impaired Pupils in Mainstream Schools*. London: David Fulton.

Webster, A (1986) *Deafness, Development and Literacy*. London: Methuen.

Webster, A and Ellwood, J (1985) *The Hearing Impaired Child in the Ordinary School*. Beckenham, Kent: Croom Helm.

Webster, A and Wood, D (1989) *Special Needs in Ordinary Schools: Children with Hearing Difficulties*. London: Cassell.

Wood, D, Wood, H, Griffiths, A and Howarth, I (1986) *Teaching and Talking with Deaf Children*. Chichester: Wiley.

Useful Resources

Ewing Foundation, Centre for Audiology, Education of the Deaf and Speech Pathology, University of Manchester, Oxford Road, Manchester M13 9PL.

The Ewing Foundation produces a range of videos on helping pupils with hearing impairment. Details are available from the address above. They also employ education consultants who are available to offer courses to staff dealing with pupils with hearing impairment.

The RNID has produced a series of educational guidelines on working with deaf pupils. A complete list is available on their website: www.rnid.org

'No Problem?' video produced by Maud Maxfield Service, Hazelbarrow School, Hazelbarrow Crescent, Sheffield S8 8AQ.

This is a useful video for mainstream staff working with secondary-aged pupils with hearing impairment.

Many Services for Hearing Impaired Pupils have videos that can be borrowed, for more details contact your local service for hearing impaired children.

BDA (British Deaf Association), 38 Victoria Place, Carlisle CA1 1HU, produces videos on signing.

CACDP (Council for the Advancement of Communication with Deaf People), Pelaw House, School of Education, University of Durham, Durham DH1 1TA, produces training videos on signing.

Connevans Ltd, 54 Albert Road North, Reigate RH2 9YR, will supply a helpful booklet on radio hearing aids.

The National Deaf Children's Society (NDCS), 15 Dufferin Street, London EC1Y 8PD, is an association for parents of pupils with hearing impairment. It also produces literature for parents and professionals, and a magazine.

DELTA (Deaf Education through Listening and Talking), PO Box 20, Haverhill, Suffolk CB9 7BD, is an association that supports parents and professionals working with pupils with hearing impairment in oral/aural settings.

BATOD (British Association of Teachers of the Deaf), Secretary Ann Underwood, 41 The Orchard, Leven, Beverley HU17 5QA, is the professional association of teachers of the deaf. It produces a journal for teachers of the deaf.